Car

of

Pearls

Cancer Births A String of *Pearls*

Wisdom Pearls gathered in a Cancer Storm

FELIPE CHAVEZ

TATE PUBLISHING
AND ENTERPRISES, LLC

Published by Tate Publishing & Enterprises, LLC
127 E. Trade Center Terrace | Mustang, Oklahoma 73064 USA
1.888.361.9473 | www.tatepublishing.com

Tate Publishing is committed to excellence in the publishing industry. The company reflects the philosophy established by the founders, based on Psalm 68:11,
"The Lord gave the word and great was the company of those who published it."

Published in the United States of America

ISBN: 978-1-62902-881-1
1. Self-Help / Personal Growth / General
2. Self-Help / General
13.11.20

Table of Contents

Acknowledgments

Throughout the gestation, birth pangs, and final birth of this book of hope, I have been blessed by the very real presence of my wife, Loretta, who was like God's angel through each painful phase of my cancer treatment—she truly completes me!

I especially acknowledge our dearest neighbor, Laura Ann Shaffer, for patiently and lovingly editing my writing in spite of her own tough journey with Lou Gehrig's disease. She and her husband have been amazing inspirations to both me and my wife. Laura entered the beautiful presence of God on November 13, 2011. She was last seen running and skipping joyfully, amid the most glorious array of flowers in her heavenly Father's garden. A lyric from a song that was most meaningful to her is:

> The Master is seeking a harvest, in lives He's redeemed by His blood:
>
> He seeks for the fruit of the Spirit, and works that will glorify God.

Her memorial words read: "It is my fervent hope that I have delivered fruit."

From the bounds of this earthly grasp, I will raise my hands to God's heaven and shout, "Thank you, dear God, for letting us taste of the fruit of your beautiful daughter while you lent her to us."

A special thanks to my sons; Dwayne and Dean, for their love and support throughout my ordeal. I also thank God for the expanded circle of Christian brothers and sisters who daily held me and my family up to God's throne, praying that his mercy, grace, love, and healing power guide us through our journey.

Foreword

A cancer diagnosis brings everyone (patient and support group) to a critical *crossroad* in life. The word *cancer* delivers a cruel and suffocating punch of reality to our lives and threatens to kill us. Dark and hopeless agents of doom parade their deadly whispers to our brain, hoping to find a secure hold from which to drop their deadly poison to our hearts. They salivate at the chance of infecting and killing our deepest God-given treasures: faith, hope, and love.

The word *cancer* unleashes the agents to attack. They march in their hope-killing queue: anxiety, anger, bitterness, depression, fear, hopelessness, resentment, and self-pity. They have been on this parade before they know exactly what to do at our point of greatest weakness. But there is hope in our most vulnerable hour. There is a *cross* on this dark road of struggle; we are not left to fend for ourselves. In the midst of our terrifying experience, we can cry out to God for help or submit to the voices of the dark and hopeless agents of doom.

Here is what cancer *can't* do:

It can't cripple *love*.

It can't shatter hope.

It can't corrode faith.

It can't take away peace.

It can't destroy confidence.

It can't silence courage.

It can't kill friendship.

It can't suppress memories.

It can't invade the soul.

Cancer is very limited!

I believe God has enabled me to bring you this book of hope to help you pick the right road at whatever crossroad of pain or hopelessness you may be experiencing in your life.

Have you ever wondered where spiritual inspiration comes from? What is it? you may ask. Can I get in line to get my portion? you might wonder. The answer can sometimes be found smack in the middle of the abandonment of our own agenda and selfish desires and trusting God for his outcome of whatever trials, tribulations, or life 101 painful issues we may currently face.

How do I abandon myself? you might ask. Good question, I'll give you my personal opinion. It is truly different for each person, specifically because we are uniquely created and gifted by our Creator. All I can share is that my abandonment came during chemotherapy treatment for stage I non-Hodgkin's lymphoma cancer. In reality, self-abandonment is truly an oxymoron since self never gives up of its own selfish accord.

Somewhere in the midst of the debilitating chemo routine, where love and constant prayer by family and friends are the only oasis to drink from, I discovered my moment of abandonment. I chose to trust God for whatever outcome he chose for me. In that precious moment when I came with no agenda, other than I needed to be loved in my storm of life, I whispered, "I love you, Jesus. I trust you, Jesus. May your perfect will be done in my life. Bring honor and glory to your name through my storm." I chose to cling to the Cross at my painful crossroad in life, and it was my salvation—whether I lived or died.

You see, I've been God's child for thirty-six years, and I remember reciting a multiplicity of abandoning-self prayers, and I really meant them! Now I realize that a reluctant self, hiding in the inner shadows of my soul, never really committed self to the altar of God. But this time—this blessed time!—I honestly believe that my deceptive self, who so cleverly hid in the shadows is experiencing the fire of God's altar—*whoosh!*

Does this mean I'm perfect? Certainly not! Do I still struggle daily? Certainly! But I now know that one of the pearls I am taking away from this experience is a profound clarity of Christ in me!

Another pearl that I'm carrying away from this experience is the creation testimony, stories that I call *A Blessed String of Pearls*. These stories came by inspiration during long sleepless post-chemo nights when I walked the hallway doubled over in pain with an eerie, painful, guttural groan, which escaped my parched lips in rhythm to my every step. These dark nights of the body and soul where death almost seems a relief are very real. But don't give up hope, child, cling to Jesus as I did, and ask him to carry you in the storm.

I believe that God used this painful part of my life to place his holy finger on a writing gift he had deposited in me long ago to inspire you. These inspirational accounts are meant to birth the rise of hope and faith in an otherwise hopeless and painful time in your life. Did you get that? This fresh gift is meant for you, the reader. Enjoy!

May the Holy God, who set fire to my reluctant self, keep that beast at bay as I write these point-of-view creation testimonies. May all the glory and honor return to God, who gifted me to gift you, my patient readers.

Introduction

Aliveness of Creation

As humans, we so easily get wrapped up in ourselves and our techno-gadgets (iPad, iPhone, Internet, etc.), we really begin to believe that it is truly all about us! An article in *The Washington Post* told about a fifteen-year-old girl who sent and received 6,473 cell phone messages in a single month. She says about her constant communication with friends, "I would die without it." And she is not alone. Researchers say that US teens with cell phones average more than 2,200 text messages a month.

To me, this ongoing digital conversation offers a remarkable illustration of what prayer could and should be like for every follower of Christ. Paul, the apostle, seemed to be constantly in an attitude of prayer for others:

> We do not cease to pray for you.
>
> Colossians 1:9

> Praying always with all prayer and supplication in the Spirit.
>
> Ephesians 6:18

> Pray without ceasing.
>
> Thessalonians 5:15

But how can we possibly do that? A certain missionary, Frank Laubach, described his habit of "shooting" prayers at people as he encountered them during the course of each day. In a sense, he was "texting" God on their behalf, staying in constant communication with the Father.

We've lost that awesome wonder of looking up at the millions of stars, planets, and galaxies majestically flung into space by our creator with one phrase, "Let there be light." We have accepted the mundane Pavlovian-like response to the myriad of techno-gadgets that demand that we answer the text, get our mail, and update Facebook. Me! Me! Me! It's all about me! Surely, I'm not the only person who sees this happening all around us. Is anyone awake? There is an upside benefit to the techno devices in our lives, but did we notice when the line was crossed? When did these devices cease to be a beneficial service and begin demanding our attention (akin to Pavlov's dog experiment)? And at what point did we become the response to their stimuli? Do we own them and use them, or do they demand our ownership and abuse us?

Is there a downside to all this me-centered madness? Well, I'm glad I asked. The Bible records the following in Romans 1:18–22:

> For the wrath of God is revealed from heaven against all ungodliness and unrighteousness of men who suppress the truth in unrighteousness, because what may be known of God is manifest in them, for God has shown it to them. For since the creation of the world,

His invisible attributes are clearly seen, being understood by the things that are made, even His eternal
power and Godhead, so that they are without excuse,
because although they knew God, they did not glorify
Him as God, nor were thankful, but became futile in
their thoughts, and their foolish hearts were darkened.
Professing to be wise they became fools.

Social media devices possess the ability to captivate our
attention downward to serve them while focusing on inflat-
ing self, increasingly at the expense of loved ones. Their ulti-
mate goal is to steal our hearts and attention away from each
other and from seeking God's plan for our lives.

In these stories of hope, I believe God is calling us to wake
up and appreciate the majestic and awe-inspiring creative
wonders that surround us daily. There will be a final test (judgment) on our choice. In Isaiah 55:6–12, the Bible records:

Seek the Lord while He may be found, call upon
Him while He is near. Let the wicked forsake his
way, and the unrighteous man his thoughts; let him
return to the Lord and He will have mercy on him;
and to our God, for He will abundantly pardon. "For
My thoughts are not your thoughts, nor are your ways
My ways, says the Lord. For as the heavens are higher
than the earth, so are My ways higher than your ways,
and My thoughts than your thoughts. For as the rain
comes down, and the snow from heaven, And do not
return there, But water the earth, And make it bring
forth and bud, That it may give seed to the sower and

bread to the eater, So shall My word be that goes forth from My mouth; It shall not return to Me void, But it shall accomplish what I please, And it shall prosper in the thing for which I sent it. "For you shall go out with joy, And be led out with peace; The mountains and the hills Shall break forth into singing before you, And all the trees of the field shall clap their hands.

Did you hear that? Mountains and hills joyfully shouting and trees clapping! Pretty awesome creative aliveness, I'd say! Now expand the above to all nature: sun, moon, stars, ocean, sea, tree, bush, grass, etc. You get the picture. There is an awesome symphony serenading our every waking second. When did we cease to hear the music? When man sinned against God, man chose to sever his perfect relationship to walk and talk with God in the Garden of Eden. The major symphony of creation that serenaded them daily was also subjected.

In Romans 8:18–23, the Bible records:

For I consider that the sufferings of this present time are not worthy to be compared with the glory which shall be revealed in us. For the earnest expectation of the creation eagerly waits for the revealing of the sons of God. For the creation was subjected to futility, not willingly, but because of Him who subjected it in hope; creation itself will be delivered from the bondage of corruption into the glorious liberty of the children of God. For we know that the whole creation groans and labors with the birth pangs together until now. Not only that, but we also who have the first fruits of the Spirit, even we ourselves groan within ourselves, eagerly awaiting for the adoption, the redemption of our body.

Author's Insight to Understanding Blessed String of Pearls

Long sleepless nights were not, in retrospect, a waste but a time of great spiritual insight. Post-chemo trauma will truly only be understood by my fellow sojourners and their support group. I don't have the liberty of blaming God for my cancer journey. Although I do understand why some people, who have yet to yield their lives to God, will blame God for all their troubles in life.

You see, thirty-six years ago, an intellectually self-absorbed egotist, who didn't believe or acknowledge God, crashed into the haunting emptiness of his own making. He cried out in desperation, "God, I have pursued the world's path to success, yet I don't have the peace promised at the end of this human pursuit. I don't even know if you exist. I don't know how to believe anymore, but if you exist, please deliver me from this self-destructive pride that has encrusted my heart in a cement tomb. Forgive my sins for they are many. Please give me a new heart!" In the next beautiful and blessed moment, I felt God's presence and forgiveness and clearly heard an audible heavenly response, "Tonight, I have given you a new heart."

Pawshunk! (Note: Author's made-up word for the sound of a piercing sword). God's Word pierced to the heart of this surrendering egotist, like a double-edged sword through the seemingly impervious cement wall that I had so carefully and ignorantly constructed around myself. Instantly, I felt the most beautiful wounding of the heart, and I knew that I would never be the same. All my life, I thought that I had to be good and perform my way to God. I did not know that all I had to do was acknowledge that I had sinned against God, turn away from sin, and accept Christ's perfect sacrifice as the redemption price God had provided for my freedom. At the age of twenty-eight, I opened my first Bible, where I read from Ephesians 2:8–9:

> For by Grace you have been saved through faith and that not of yourselves; it is the gift of God, not of works, lest anyone should boast.

Today, the same loving arms of God are cradling me, in Christ Jesus, through this journey.

On post-chemo days, while I tried to get my mind away from pain, emptiness, and a sense of abandonment, I experienced depleted energy levels. If I could have measured my energy levels with an energy meter, I would be in the extremely low range. I grasped for and was sustained by Bible memory verses, which bathed my dried-up soul with hope in a seemingly hopeless situation. I then mentally crawled into the miracle accounts of Jesus to picture what was going on and to focus my mind and body away from the very real post-chemo pain. I reread the accounts and replayed them in my mind with me on the sidelines as a curious observer during those nights where I was fortunate to get one or two hours of sleep. You see, I was extremely fortunate that these Bible accounts were there for me to search for and replay in my mind. I found myself trying to picture the supporting characters in the different scenes (not necessarily the main characters) and say to myself, "I wonder what he thought? What she thought? They thought? I wonder how and if they were affected?" Suddenly, the Spirit of God changed my view from focusing on human character viewpoints to the various supporting nonhuman creation elements that also witnessed each account.

I believe that it is from this blessed viewpoint, enabled by the Spirit of God, during my long, traumatic, and pain-racked nights that *A Blessed String of Pearls* was born. Each pearl starts and unfolds as follows:

a)   A Scripture account of a miracle of Jesus.

b)   A fictional creation witness expansion of the event, while carefully maintaining the truth of the account. These were born post-chemo session #1.

c)   A personal reflection and prayer for each account. Some of these reflections and prayers were born out of past personal experience; others were inspiration born for the express purpose of bringing freedom to your own troubled heart. These reflection/

prayer accounts were born post-chemo session #2 and #3.

I pray that God's Holy Spirit not only guides my ready pen as the pearls are hand-picked in pain, but also prepares the heart of each reader to absorb God's holy balm for the healing of your own wounded hearts and spirits.

I sense deep within my spirit that you, my patient reader or perhaps fellow sojourner, are the benefactor of these pearl gifts. May your heart and spirit be open to whatever pearls of wisdom God may want to gift you through these inspired accounts.

My hope is that you in turn will respond to God's precious gift of love. An unconditional love that was born out of God's pain where Jesus Christ bore the penalty for our sin and released God's forgiveness and redemptive love for all mankind.

> For God so loved the world, that He gave His only begotten Son, that whomsoever believes in Him, shall not perish but have everlasting life.
>
> John 3:16

At this crossroad—Calvary's Cross—is where the shackles that held me bound in sin and hopelessness were broken and I was set free, eventually to bring you this story.

A Plank's Witness

Scripture Passage

On the same day, when evening had come. He said to them, "Let us cross over to the other side." Now when they had left the multitude, they took Him along in the boat as He was. And other little boats were also with Him. And a great windstorm arose, and the waves beat into the boat, so that it was already filling. But He was in the stern, asleep on a pillow. And they awoke Him and said to Him, "Teacher, do you not care that we are perishing?"

Then He arose and rebuked the wind and said to the sea, "Peace, be still!" And the wind ceased and there was a great calm. But He said to them, "Why are you so fearful? How is it that you have no faith?" And they feared exceedingly, and said to one another, "Who can this be, that even the wind and sea obey Him?"

Mark 4:35–41

Blessed Pearl 1 – A Plank's Witness

The moment his body melted tiredly into the back of the boat, where I serve as main support to my fellow planks,

I know instantly that creative royalty is on board. A surge of creative memory flows through me, and I have visions of being a stately tree clapping in symphony with the rest of creation, praising our God! What could this mean? I ponder as I cradle my Creator fully clothed in a man's body. I remember a story my tree parents used to tell of another plank that had the honor of cradling royalty as a baby in a manger, thirty or so years ago. Could it be? Could it possibly be that the baby is now this man I have the blessed honor of cradling in my arms?

Suddenly, the wind whips into a passionate dance, above and all around me. The sea awakes beneath me as waves proudly rise and fall in heavenward rhythm, sending their resounding splashes cascading into the boat. It seems like the wind and waves know that this man, the creative Word of God, is on board. A smile momentarily passes across the Son of Man's face as if he was thoroughly enjoying the spontaneously glorious symphony, which has so suddenly erupted in praise. My thoughts are interrupted by stumbling feet rushing toward me. A trembling hand stretches out from a stumbling fisherman's body being propelled forward by sheer panic and fear. As he falls, his outstretched hand shakes our Creator awake.

I hear someone say, "Teacher, do you not care that we are perishing?" Immediately, the Conductor of Creation raises his hand gently, quiets the wind, and says to the sea, "Peace, be still!" The wind dies down and peaceful calmness rules the day. As surely as he had spoken in creation, "Let there be light," and there was light. So here too, the Word still rules all of creation.

One moment, they were riding the crest of a high wave. Everyone on board is in fear and panic stricken, holding on to mast and fellowmen for safety in a seemingly endless storm. The very next second, sequent in perfect time order, every wide-eyed, open-mouthed person is resting in God's perfect calmness! Before they can blink or close their mouths, they hear Jesus say, "Why are you so fearful? How is it that you have no faith?" I sense a different fear, an exceedingly great awe settle over the men's faces. They say to one another, "Who can this be that even the wind and sea obey him!"

Did you notice? Did you catch this profound moment of clarity? You see, neither we the planks, the sea, the wind, nor any other creative force now joined in a calm symphony of praise wrestle with their question because we recognize the royal Word—our Creator God!

Reflection

Far too many times, Lord, I have been guilty of letting your creation landscape, which surrounds me daily, pass unnoticed in my daily grind. When my life seems functionally sound (work, play, family, health), I must consciously reason that I have created the stability. Where did my childlike wonder, awe, and faith get swallowed up and replaced with a stark black-and-white house of false reality? A proud house I constructed using my ego and society's values as a foundation. Now these murky and ashen-grey windows keep me from seeing or enjoying your creation's splendor and from needing or seeking you.

The trials and pain of life's uncertainty fuel the cruel winds that blow and shake my boat: job loss, sickness, alcoholism, drug addiction, and death. I frantically run to those now dark grey windows. I rub vigorously in panic for some source of hope, but to no avail. I'm trapped in the house of me!

Personal Prayer

I'm crying, Lord, do you see me? Lord, with childlike fear, wonder, and a seed of faith from yesteryear's child, I'm crying in desperation. Do you hear me? Do you not care that I am perishing? I feel your presence as you now whisper, "Why are you so fearful? How is it you have no faith?"

Lord, I feel tears now stream uncontrollably down my face. I realize that those dark, ashen windows are my eyes of faith that I carelessly and methodically traded for a reasoned worldview. A worldview that propagates Godlessness and whose goal is to erase you from the world you created.

Forgive me, Lord, for trading you away at the world's doorstep. Forgive me for ignoring your Word, which states in 1 John 2:15:

> Do not love the world or the things in the world. If anyone loves the world the love of the Father is not in him. For all that is in the world—the lust of the flesh, the lust of the eyes, and the pride of life—is not of the Father but is of the world. And the world is passing away, and the lusts thereof; but he who does the will of God abides forever.

I now see where the deceptive worldview has led me—away from you! I now choose with this newfound faith to seek your purpose and will for my life. Pain, failure, and sorrow in my personal life have served to awaken faith in me. Thank you, dear God, for opening my eyes of faith. I can see clearly now the stain is gone.

A Fish's Witness

Scripture Passage

When they had come to Capernaum, those who received the temple tax came to Peter and said, "Does your Teacher not pay the temple tax?" He said, "Yes." And when he had come into the house, Jesus anticipated him, saying, "What do you think, Simon? From whom do the kings of the earth take customs or taxes, from their sons or from strangers?" Peter said to Him, "From strangers."

Jesus said to him, "Then the sons are free. Nevertheless, lest we offend them, go to the sea, cast in a hook, and take the fish that comes up first. And when you have opened its mouth, you will find a piece of money; take that and give it to them for me and you."

Matthew 17:24-27

Blessed Pearl 2 – Above the Sea (Background to Fish Witness)

As a Roman official is being ferried across the Sea of Galilee, one of his centurions asks, "Excellency, what do you make of all this Jewish talk of a Messiah who walks among them?" The Roman official stands and purposely picks two contrasting coins from his money bag: a Roman denarius and a Jewish shekel. He then pompously states, "Unlike the denarius, which bears our great Caesar's image and who is truly the ruler and god of this world, this Jewish shekel (along with the Jewish vermin who coined it) will perish along with their messiah."

He pauses briefly, looks toward Rome, takes a deep breath, and says, "Long live, Caesar," as he pounds his chest in allegiance. The trained voices of subordinates respond in obligatory cue, "Long live, Caesar." Then with a dismissive flick of his thumb against his finger, the Roman official tosses the shekel high into the sunlit morning air.

Suddenly, a piercing ray of sunlight ricochets off the falling shekel and shines back into the Roman official's eyes. He recoils and shields his eyes from the precise ray of sunlight that momentarily blinds him. As a wind gust brushes across his face, little does he realize that he has just made provision to pay the temple tax for a lowly fisherman *and* the Jewish Messiah. Christ the Messiah that he had so arrogantly dismissed in the sight of heaven. The gold shekel pierces the water's surface and disappears.

Below the Sea — A Fish's Witness

I, a hungry fish, swim by in search of food and I'm attracted to a tumbling bright tidbit. "Aha, come to Papa," I state as I dive, gulp, and immediately try to spit out my strange catch. Again, I try to spit, but to no avail. Whatever it is—it is firmly lodged between my teeth and jaw.

Suddenly, another flashing swoosh pierces the water, and before I know it, my lower lip is being pulled upward at a massive pace toward the light. As I break the surface of the water, I suddenly find myself in the calloused hand of a seasoned fisherman. I feel an unusually tender finger and thumb remove the hook from my lip and dislodge the impediment. "Praise God, Praise God!" I hear the fisherman yell joyously heavenward. With a flip of the fisherman's hand, I find myself flying above the Sea of Galilee. "Wow, what a tremendous view of creation, and here I thought I had seen it all." Splash! I hit the water and propel myself back to the safety of my known world.

"Whew, what a day!" I've experienced a whole new side of creation I never knew existed. "Thank you, Creator, for allowing me the honor of witnessing for you!"

Reflection

In my "make it easy on yourself" world, I would have preferred that you, Jesus, would have pulled the coin out of Peter's big ear. Saves time and entertains the crowd.

Then again, I realize that I sometimes treat you as if you were my own personal genie, here specifically to do my bidding on my timetable.

When did I become so faithless and anchored to my own selfish comfort and expectations that I forgot how to walk in obedience and patience? Perhaps I've imagined a god of my own making, ending up with myself as god, simply because I dared to define you in my own rebellious and self-serving image.

More times than not, I act like the proud Roman official depending only on self and marching in allegiance to a worldview whose sole purpose is to serve government as their god. A false god who legalizes ungodly behavior and excludes any dependence or reliance on the one true God—their creator!

Personal Prayer

Forgive me for the times that my belief and allegiance to you has been as shallow as the puddle that wet Peter's sandals as he ran in faith to obey your command. For those insincere brief sporadic moments when I threw up a desperate prayer that was motivated by self-preservation—I knew it and you knew it, yet you saw me through my dilemma.

I need you, God, to deliver me from my own personal agenda and ungodly dependence on self-performance when it comes to a sincere relationship with you. I ask in faith that you penetrate my heart with your word, which states, "Be anxious for nothing, but in everything by prayer and supplication, with thanksgiving, let your requests be made known to God; and the peace of God which surpasses all understanding, will guard your hearts and minds through Christ Jesus" (Philippians 4:6).

Help me depend on you and to serve you with a renewed heart of obedience, a heart untarnished by the deceptive lies of this world. Help me to be honest and thankful for all the blessings in my life. I trust that your peace will guard my heart and mind in Christ Jesus. Amen.

A Sound Wave's Witness

Now they came to Jericho. As he went out of Jericho with his disciples and a great multitude, blind Bartimaeus, the son of Timaeus, sat by the road begging. And when he heard that it was Jesus of Nazareth, he began to cry out and say, "Jesus, Son of David, have mercy on me!"

Then many warned him to be quiet, but he cried out all the more, "Son of David, have mercy on me!" So Jesus stood still and commanded him to be called. Then they called the blind man, saying to him, "Be of good cheer. Rise, he is calling you." And throwing aside his garment, he rose and came to Jesus. So Jesus answered and said to him, "What do you want me to do for you?"

The blind man said to him, "Rabboni, that I may receive my sight." Then Jesus said to him, "Go your way, your faith has made you well." And immediately, he received his sight and followed Jesus on the road.

Mark 10:46–52

Blessed Pearl 3 — A Sound Wave's Witness

As the traveling merchant glances back to search for the origin of all the excitement coming out of Jericho, his eyes lock on Jesus in the center of the multitude. Seems like only a short time back, as he was peddling his wares in the Decapolis area, he had the blessed privilege of listening to Jesus teach another multitude of people in this same wilderness. He remembered hanging on to every word as Jesus taught. He vividly recalls the miracle Jesus had performed that day, feeding 4,000 people by multiplying seven fish and a few loaves of bread. The traveler took a deep breath as he formed his lips to speak and propelled me (a sound wave) into the air.

I vibrate with excitement as I bounce and reverberate toward and into the ear drum of a blind beggar named Bartimaeus. I deliver the words in sequence, "Jesus of Nazareth is coming." Hope rises in Bartimaeus and gives spring to faith as he cries out, "Jesus Son of David, have mercy on me." The sound of his first cry is cancelled and deadened by many opposing cries shouting back, "Be quiet!" Bartimaeus's faith will not be denied. He takes a deep, deep breath and expels another persistent cry, "Jesus, Son of David, have mercy on me!" The powerful surge of his faithful cry sends the hopeful plea, on wings of sound waves, to the ears of Jesus, and he comes to a standstill, as does the multitude around him.

The silence of hundreds of sandaled feet coming to a stop in unison is like music to the blind beggar's ear. He now trembles with hopeful anticipation. A cry of faith will always reach the ears of Jesus. Jesus commands the same men, who originally told the beggar to be quiet, to bring Bartimaeus to him. Bartimaeus then hears approaching footsteps. Suddenly, another sound wave reverberates in his ear, conveying the message, "Be of good cheer. Rise, Jesus is calling you." Excitedly, he rises and throws aside his garment, revealing the boney outline of his beggarly frame. With outstretched boney arms and spindly legs, he moves toward Jesus. The crowd opens a path about a person wide, which serves as a guide for the wispy-framed sightless beggar to feel his way onward to Jesus. A disciple's arm across his rib bone–defined chest lets the beggar know that he has reached his destination.

A blessed moment of silence loudly defines a blessed destiny as another majestically welcome sound wave, like nothing he has ever heard in his life, travels to his ear and bounces to his heart, embracing the source of his faithful cry. "What do you want me to do for you?" Bartimaeus replies, "Rabboni, that I might receive sight." At close range, waves of faith are now operating in heavenly ordained sequence as Jesus says, "Go your way, your faith has made you well." The power of the spoken Living Word powerfully carries the creative life-giving message to Bartimaeus, and a blessed miracle takes place! Two sets of eyes were opened that day for Bartimaeus. His physical eyes were likely opened at the same time. The outward healing reflected the inner wellness of salvation. Bartimaeus's first glimpse *ever* is bathed with grateful tears of joy and awe. His eyes are fixed on Jesus's face, framing eyes of compassion and a broad, faith-affirming smile. The heretofore insignificant beggar in people's eyes has become significant in God's eyes as he embraces faith and is made whole. Immediately, he follows Jesus down the road, taking in every majestic color of God's creation, an awesome array of colors that had long ago ceased to bring awe to those who could see.

The sound wave recalls a majestic memory of a time 1,430 years ago, in this very same place (Jericho), when God's people shouted in orderly obedient faith and the walls of Jericho came tumbling down (Joshua 6:20).

Reflection

Sometimes, in my quiet reflective times, in the early morning hours, before the demands and expectations of the upcoming day set me on my habitual performance routines, I hear your voice gently calling me out of this earthly self-imposed grave of religious performance to a higher level of compassion and love.

Standing in the intersection, she holds a sign that reads: "Please help. Out of work. Baby needs milk. God bless!" I look. I see. I read. I judge. I pass by, unmoved by her plea. Although I say nothing, I'm like the people in this account as I think without saying, "Be quiet, don't bother me, for heaven's sake—get a job!"

When did my own heart become such a compassionless void? My uncaring, self-serving heart has ceased to be moved by the needs of my fellowmen. I've become a blind and dead man walking. Is there hope for me?

Personal Prayer

Dear Jesus, ask me, ask me, please. Ask me, "What do you want me to do for you?" I will say, "I am so prone to judge some people as insignificant that I have become blind. Open the eyes of my heart, open my heart! I've caught a glimpse of my compassionless heart and it terrifies me!"

Please fill me with your Spirit. Fill me with your love and compassion. Help me throw aside my garment of judgment and clothe me with your holy discernment that I may see that all people are significant in your sight.

Give me grace to live out my significance and new life in Christ by helping others to see a glimpse of your pure and perfect love in spite of my own frailties. I thank you, dear God, that through the resurrection power of Jesus Christ in my life that I can make a difference in the life of people you bring into my life. In your precious name I pray. Amen.

The Dust Witness

But Jesus went to the Mount of Olives. Now early in the morning He came again into the temple, and all the people came to Him; and He sat down and taught them. Then the Scribes and Pharisees bought to Him a woman caught in adultery. And when they had set her in their midst, they said to Him. "Teacher, this woman was caught in adultery, in the very act.

Now Moses in the law, commanded us that such should be stoned. But what do You say?" This they said, testing Him that they might have something of which to accuse Him. But Jesus stooped down and wrote on the ground with His finger, as though He did not hear. So, when they continued asking Him. He raised Himself up and said to them, "He who is without sin among you, let him throw a stone at her first."

And again He stooped down and wrote on the ground. Then those who heard it, being convicted by their conscience, went out one by one, beginning with the oldest even to the last. And Jesus was left alone, and the woman standing in the midst. When Jesus had raised Himself up and saw no one but the woman He said to her; "Woman, where are those accusers of yours? Has no one condemned you?" She said, "No one,

Lord." And Jesus said to her, "Neither do I condemn you; go and sin no more."

John 8:1–11

Blessed Pearl 4 — The Dust Witness

As a ground mixture of dirt and crushed pebbles, I anchor the feet of all temple visitors. Today, I am again honored to support the sandals and weight of Jesus of Nazareth and listen to the same creative Word of God teach the people as the Feast of Tabernacles comes to a close.

I, dust, am a credible witness since I preceded man in God's creative order. I'll set forth how I preceded man and subsequently was used by God in the creation of man on the sixth day:

> So God created man in His own image; in the image of God He created him; male and female He created them.

Genesis 1:27

So here's where I come in. The Bible further records:

> And the Lord God formed man of the *dust* of the ground and breathed life into his nostrils, the breath of life, and man became a living being.

Genesis 2:7

The Pharisees and Sadducees plot all through the feast to have the temple guard officers arrest Jesus. They see Jesus as a threat to their established religious and political power. The Pharisees were a small legalistic sect of the Jews who were known for their rigid adherence to the ceremonial fine points of the law. The Sadducees were known for their denial of things supernatural. They denied the resurrection of the dead and the existence of angels. Unlike the Pharisees, they rejected human tradition and scorned legalism. Normally politically and religiously at odds, they united together in their opposition of Jesus.

Jesus continued teaching:

> Therefore, many from the crowd, when they heard this saying, said: Truly this is the Prophet. Others said, This is the Christ (Messiah).

John 7:40

When the officers return empty-handed, they were met with stern-eyed glares from the religious hierarchy.

> Then the officers came to the Chief Priests and Pharisees, who said to them, " Why have you not brought Him?" The officers answered, "No man ever spoke like this Man!"

John 7:45–46

There was much turmoil in the temple area this week as the sandals of angry, religious factions and supporters of Christ kicked and tossed me (dust) all over the place. As I settled back to the earth, I asked myself, "When did the purity and image of God begin to dissipate so badly in man?"

Today, as Jesus teaches, all is calm. Suddenly, I'm again being disturbed by an angry parade of Pharisee sandals, dragging a half-naked woman. I feel the upper part of her bare feet skimming on my surface, as I'm forced into the spaces between her toes. The woman is set center stage: trembling, hair disheveled, makeup scrambled and caked on her face with tears and dust.

The angry, self-righteous, accusatory voices say, in essence, "We pulled this woman from underneath the man she was sinning with." The woman is looking down at me in shame, quite unlike the proud, beautifully adorned temptress she had allowed herself to become. The Pharisees continue to righteously rant about how Mosaic Law says she must be stoned. They then smugly await the snap of their preset word trap as they ask, "What do you say?" The Pharisees' rationale in setting the trap was if Jesus rejected the law of Moses, his credibility would be gone. If he upheld to Mosaic law, his reputation for compassion would be in question.

I feel my Creator's weight shift as he stoops down and runs his finger across me (dust). Memories of creation time past, when holy hands formed me into original man, explode within me. I feel the sacred finger of my Creator writing on my surface in peaceful, broad, caressing strokes. He is seemingly oblivious of the angry accusers, whose clenched, reddened hands are a pressure point away from crushing the very stones they hold in righteous indignation.

I feel the impatient, shuffling sandals and hear the angry mob repeat their case for stoning as they raise their stones in anticipation of Jesus's answer. Once again, I feel my Creator's weight shift as he raises himself up and looks directly into every eye in the mob as he says, "He who is without sin among you, let him throw a stone at her first." Jesus then stooped down to me again and resumed writing.

Instantly, the God-empowered Word that Jesus has spoken hits the heart of every stone-bearing man and convicts him. The truth of the Word that has been God empowered since the beginning of time would eventually be recorded as follows:

> For the Word of God is living and powerful, and sharper than any two-edged sword, piercing even to the division of soul and spirit, and of joints and marrow, and is a discerner of the thoughts and intents of the heart. And there is no creature hidden from His sight, but all things are naked and open to the eyes of Him whom we must give account.
>
> Hebrews 4:12–13

Meanwhile, all the stone holders, who experienced eye contact with the perfect justice, love, and forgiveness of God in Jesus's eyes experienced the double-edged sword of conviction right to the heart. Almost instantaneously, the same powerful sword pierces and resonates deep within the heart of the half-naked adulteress convicting her of her sin. She sobs silently inside herself as she realizes the burden of her sin. She waits in fearful expectation of her impending stoning, yet somehow knows that she stands before the compassionate True Judge of all mankind.

Suddenly, the oldest Pharisee drops his stone, which leaves a crater on my surface, with a loud thud. The half-naked woman at center stage winces in fear as if she just escaped a direct hit by a bad-aiming Pharisee. One by one, I feel a dust explosion as stones fall into my surface in a chorus of thuds. One by one, all of the accusers turn and leave. With each resounding thud, the woman's body convulses in panic and then relief as nary a stone hits her.

I sense my Creator raise himself up and he sees no one but the woman. He says to her, "Woman, where are those accuser of yours? Has no one condemned you?" She says, "No one, Lord." And Jesus said to her, "Neither do I condemn you. Go and sin no more."

I had been cradling her bare feet. and I feel the downward pressure lighten tremendously as the word "Lord" comes trembling from her lips. As Jesus forgives her, I sense a holy groundswell of mercy as forgiveness sets her free. Her tears of repentance drop and embrace me. I collapse gently into each beautiful tear. For precious moments, I share the joyous elation of her spiritual rebirth.

Reflection

I also disguise myself at times like the Pharisee and the adulteress in this account. I can be a critical, self-righteous person demanding my form of justice. I may not physically picked up a stone to toss, but demanding and destructive words have certainly flown out of my mouth. I have cruelly impaled and blistered many a heart with a spiteful, angry, and bitter lash of my tongue.

I am also capable of preening at length—disguising myself as the well-dressed, sweet-smelling, and pleasing adulteress in this account. While all the time, I'm hiding in my own cave of darkness and wounded self-worth. I feel a deep-rooted unworthiness blistering my heart.

I'm tired of donning disguises for each occasion simply to please others. I'm not only falsely elevating myself with deceitful lies, but truth be known, most people can see right through my transparent masks.

Personal Prayer

Lord, I pray that you will deliver me from self-righteousness and from donning deceptive disguises to present a more likeable me. I've allowed myself to be defined by the slow, painful, blistering, and cruel messengers of pain in my life. I've allowed the blisters to painfully fester in my heart and define the core of who I am. In dark and storm-driven times in my life, I've believed the lying accusatory and sinister voices which whisper, "You are unworthy of God's love!"

The freeing echo of your final words from the woman's account have resounded loudly in my own heart, "Neither do I condemn you. Go and sin no more." As a result, hope has given way to faith inside of me. Free me from my self-imposed sentence where I function as both captive and jailer, all to my own detriment and continued self-imprisonment.

Jesus, compassionate, loving, and forgiving judge, deliver me! Forgive me! Perform radical love surgery on my blistered heart. I give you permission to burst every inflamed and throbbing blister of hurt, pain, and disappointment in my heart.

I thank you. For now I know by faith that I can trust you to forgive me. Thank you for applying the balm of your soothing grace, forgiveness, and mercy to my wounded heart.

I am now worthy because you have redeemed me. Clothe me with your Holy Spirit that I might walk in your redemptive love. Amen!

An Ant's Witness

Scripture Passage

So He came to a city of Samaria which is called Sychar, near the plot of ground that Jacob gave to his son Joseph. Now Jacob's well was there. Jesus therefore, being wearied from His journey, sat thus by the well. It was about the sixth hour. A woman of Samaria came to draw water. Jesus said to her, "Give Me a drink." For His disciples had gone away into the city to buy food.

Then the woman of Samaria said to Him, "How is it that You, being a Jew, ask a drink from me, a Samaritan woman?" For Jews have no dealings with Samaritans. Jesus answered and said to her, "If you knew the gift of God, and who it is who says to you, 'Give Me a drink,' you would have asked Him, and He would have given you living water." The woman said to Him, "Sir, You have nothing to draw with and the well is deep. Where then do you get that living water? Are You greater than our father Jacob, who gave us the well, and drank from it himself, as well as his sons and his livestock?"

Jesus answered and said to her, 'whoever drinks of this water will thirst again, but whoever drinks of the water that I shall give him will never thirst. But the water that I shall give him will become in him a fountain of water springing up into everlasting life." The woman said to Him, "Sir, give me the water, that I may not thirst, nor come here to draw." Jesus said to her, "Go call your husband, and come here." The woman answered and said, "I have no husband." Jesus said to her, "You have well said, 'I have no husband,' for you have had five husbands, and the one whom you now have is not your husband; in that you spoke truly."

The woman said to Him, "Sir, I perceive that You are a prophet. Our father worshiped on this mountain and you Jews say that in "Jerusalem is the place where one ought to worship." Jesus said to her, "Woman believe Me, the hour is coming when you will neither on this mountain, nor in Jerusalem worship the Father. You worship what you do not know, we know what we worship, for salvation is of the Jews. But the hour is coming, and now is, when the true worshipers will worship the Father in spirit and truth; for the Father is seeking such to worship Him.

God is Spirit and those who worship Him must worship in spirit and truth." The woman said to Him, "I know that Messiah is coming" (who is called Christ). "When He comes, He will tell us all things." Jesus said to her, "I who speak to you am He."

John 4:5–36

Blessed Pearl 5 — An Ant's Witness

A small ant methodically zigzags his pear-shaped body across a large flat rock in search of water. A barrier blocks his path. He zigs left and zags right, only to find himself without direct passage. Now slightly frustrated, he climbs on a rough leather surface. He makes his way up, then down the side of a narrow strap and lands on flesh.

Immediately, power rushes up his six highly sensitive and strong legs and through his small body. Instinctively, he knows he is on board his Creator's foot; he senses the holy vibration of a journey-wearied voice say, "Give me a drink." Just as the ant thinks, *I'm too tiny to give you a drink*, he hears a woman's voice respond, "How is it that you being a Jew, ask a drink from me, a Samaritan woman?" My Creator then shoots straight for her heart as he says, "If you knew the gift of God and who it is who says to you, 'Give me a drink,' you would have asked him and he would have given you living water."

The woman, still preoccupied with drawing up the well water, attempts to educate Jesus through a logical and theological chess-like game of words based on her knowledge of the source of the well and her belief system.

The ant relishes his front row seat on Jesus's foot as the chess match unfolds. Chess game on! The woman moves first (paraphrase), "You have no bucket to draw with, and the well is deep." Jesus counters spiritually (paraphrase), "The water you drink will make you thirst again, but whoever drinks of the water that I give will never thirst. The water I give shall become like a fountain springing up unto everlasting life." The woman is yet to realize that Jesus, the source of living water, will soon checkmate her heart. Her material mind selfishly says, "Sir, give me this water that I may not thirst nor come here to draw."

My six sensitive feet feel my Creator's blood flow through his foot vein as he mines deeper into the spiritual depth of the woman's heart." I turn my little ant head toward the woman as she responds, "I have no husband." Strange turn of events, I think to myself as Jesus says (paraphrase), "Well said, you have no husband. In truth, you have had five husbands and the current one is not your husband." My ant jaw drops at Jesus's revelation—five husbands!

The woman's heart and conscience momentarily yield the first fruit as she states, "Sir, I perceive that you are a prophet," but her mind blocks a deeper heart response. She regresses into her cement-like belief system response as to the proper place to worship God. Jesus counters (paraphrase): "Woman, believe me, worship to the Father is not about mountains or Jerusalem. The hour is coming, and this is your hour, child, when true worshipers will worship the Father in spirit and truth."

I swivel my head toward the woman as she again religiously responds, "I know that Messiah is coming. When he comes, he will tell us all things." Tears flow down my face, I want to cry out, "Wake up, woman. I'm standing on your Messiah's foot!" The final arrow of truth hits and pierces the seemingly impervious, self-righteous, religious crust surrounding her heart. Checkmate! The truth has found her heart as she yields to the author of love. "You shall know the Truth and the Truth will set you free" (John 8:32).

I see the woman abandon her bucket, run to the city, and spread the good news. The Bible record states, "And many of the Samaritans of that city believed in Him because of the word of the woman's testimony" (John 4:39).

A warming sensation envelopes my ant frame as the tender fingers of my Creator pick me up gently and bring me close to his face. I look into his loving eyes. He smiles and gently coaxes me down his finger toward a small droplet of water as he says, "Drink, my little friend." I drink as my mind replays every minute memory of this day. I can't wait to get back to my colony to tell them this amazing story.

Jesus, at the Samaritan's bidding, stayed in the city two days, and many of the citizens with open hearts came to hear truth, to experience inner freedom, and to obtain everlasting life (John 4:41–42).

Reflection

Like the woman in this account, I, too, want an easy and lasting solution to quell the myriad of thirsts within me. At times, my dark, innermost ghosts of past actions and behaviors haunt me unceasingly by replaying shamefully defining scenes of my life. I have bartered for or blindly accepted the cunning lies of this world. I have rebelliously ignored the conscience you created within me to guide me through life.

As I reflect on my life now, with a twice empty hollowness in my blistered heart, I realize that I have been looking for love and acceptance everywhere but where I can really find them. I've followed many self-made paths, but they all turned out to be dead ends. I've settled for lustful, fleeting, and deceptive moments of self-fulfillment. I've pandered to myself at the altar of self-satisfaction by pursuing the lusts of my: flesh, eyes, and boastful pride of life. What I perceived in my yesterdays as a free-thinking, socially acceptable, and politically correct path to happiness in life, I now find has left me drawing from the empty wells of this world's false promises.

I now understand, through the above account, that it was never about "material" well water. It was all about God sending mercy and grace, in the form of Jesus, to recover a twice outcast and shunned woman (shamed by her own people and virtually nonexistent to the Jews).

I, too, feel pain and inner shunning, just like the woman at the well. I painfully don my deceptive disguises, so that I may obtain self-worth from the world at large. I've imploded into my own cavern of self-deception and I'm ready for a deep drink of spiritual truth.

Personal Prayer

Help me, Lord! I now see my true, innermost need. Forgive my rebellious and self-seeking ways. I give you permission to spiritually blast through my false fronts, and I ask you to give me a drink of your truth. The same drink of truth that found the woman of Samaria and set her free also has the awesome and powerful capacity to find me, unshackle me, and truly set me free. I have found out the hard way that my plans for my life has left me empty and wandering aimlessly through life. I give you permission to turn my life inside out and give me the grace and mercy to accept your plan for my life rather than my plan for my life.

Now that I have come to know and experience the deep hollowness and deception of my way of life, I am ready to drink of the true spiritual water that only Jesus can provide. Truly, I now understand the meaning of the following Scripture that states: "Do not love the world or the things of the world. If anyone loves the world the love of the Father is not in him. For all that is in the world—the lust of the flesh, the lust of the eyes, and the pride of life—is not of the Father but is of the world. And the world is passing away, and the lust thereof; but he who does the will of God abides forever" (1 John 2:15).

Thank you, dearest Father, for redeeming me from this world's bondage and relentless self-debasing shame and into your loving arms of mercy, forgiveness, and grace. Amen!

A Pebble Witness

Now a certain woman had a flow of blood for twelve years, and had suffered many things from many physicians. She had spent all that she had and was not better, but rather grew worse. When she heard about Jesus she came behind Him in the crowd and touched His garment. For she said, "If only I may touch His clothes, I shall be made well." Immediately the fountain of her blood was dried up, and she felt in her body that she was healed of the affliction.

And Jesus, immediately knowing in Himself that power had gone out of Him, turned around in the crowd and said, "Who touched My clothes?" But His disciples said to Him, "You see the multitude thronging You and You say, "Who touched Me?" And He looked around to see her who had done this thing. But the woman, fearing and trembling, knowing what had happened to her, came and fell down before Him and told Him the whole truth, And He said to her, "Daughter, your faith has made you well. "Go in peace, and be healed of your affliction."

Mark 5:25–34

Blessed Pearl 6 — A Pebble's Witness

A crowd moves from the northwest shore of the Sea of Galilee toward a well-traveled road. Ground surface sounds change as a multitude of sandals enter the main roadway, some still damp from seawater.

As one of many pebbles scattered on the road, I help maintain a robust, even surface. Suddenly, in the midst of the multitude of sandal presses, I sense a most holy press. I'm lodged in a small cavity on a sandal bottom.

Creation recall power awakens within me. I now realize that I'm traveling with God's Son, my creative agent. Jesus and I travel along the roadway, encircled by his disciples and thronged about by an ever-growing crowd. The crowd surges forward, pressing against a disciple who momentarily holds on to Jesus for balance. Jesus shifts his weight to provide balance for his disciple as I'm dislodged and tumble on the roadway. I feel the absence of my Creator immediately, but still sense his heightened creative presence in me.

Sandals continue their pressing march upon and past me as I'm kicked about the roadway. Suddenly, the much lighter step of a woman presses me into a nook on the bottom of her sandal. Although the step is lighter, her immense burden of physical, spiritual and emotional solitude vibrates through her body down to her feet. Her physical affliction has caused much suffering for twelve long years and an unending parade of physicians have left her hopeless and without money.

Worse than her suffering, empty purse, and distrust of man is the worthlessness of self, which had been dealt to her by men wrongfully misrepresenting God's law. The Jewish religion has become so oriented to outward performance that it has come to the point where mercy, grace, and love are excluded by man. So much so that this suffering woman was shunned by all including her own family.

Hope resurrects in her heart as she hears about Jesus and how his love, mercy, and grace extends beyond man's rigid religious borders. At sandal bottom, I now sense a strong resurgent faith and determined purpose with her every step. Powered exclusively by faith, she methodically moves forward through the outer crowd and into the inner disciple circle. With every step, I get a glimpse of a steady stream of blood drops, leaving a trail behind us.

She reaches her right hand between two disciples. I sense the faith vibration of her thoughts as she nears her target: "If only I may touch his clothes, I shall be made well." Her hand now lightly touches Jesus's garment.

Faith touches love! Love responds to faith and healing power flows. Immediately, the fountain of her blood dries up. An inner warmth flows throughout her body. The True Physician has put an end to her affliction. The steady trail of blood drops haunt us no longer!

Jesus stops. He knows that divine healing power has flowed from himself, in response to a faith call embraced by his Father. The crowd, which had been moving in unison like a swarm of bees, surges and jerks to a sandal-crowding stop. I, still embedded in the woman's sandal, feel the radiating power of Jesus on the woman like a warm fire in the crowd.

A holy silence now permeates the crowd as Jesus says, "Who touched my clothes?" His disciples' faces, all framed with quizzical looks, respond, "You see the multitude throng you, and you say, 'Who touched me?'" Jesus looks past his disciples and his loving eyes lock on the woman standing radiantly in the crowd. I feel a holy tremble and awe overtake the woman as the King of Truth calls out truth.

The disciples' inner circle parts as the woman advances and falls down before Jesus—the True Physician. She tearfully tells Jesus the whole truth. Her now bent sandal sends me flying from my nook. Jesus smiles as he looks upon the woman's tear-stained face. He then says, "Daughter, your faith has made you well. Go in peace, and be healed of your affliction." Suddenly, the woman's second and more important healing takes place: the healing of her heart. The Physician of Truth's Word comes to fruition, "And you shall know the truth, and the truth shall make you free" (John 8:32).

As she experiences her blessed worth through Christ, the woman's dark, invisible cloak of shunned worthlessness is put to flight by the strong wind of God's truth. A solitary tear of gratitude, for worthiness born anew, slowly travels the length of the woman's face and hesitates momentarily at the round of her chin. Then the tear drops as if in slow motion, reflecting a precious ray of sun on the way down as it bathes me, a simple yet majestic pebble with a blessed splash of God's love in a final good-bye!

Reflection

As I peer into my own past, I can vividly recall a multitude following me. I allowed this multitude to shape and define my self-worth. Significant people in my life spoke words, which afflicted the very core of my heart—some for better and some for worse. Sometimes deservingly as I rebelled and pushed the limits of authority. Other times undeservingly as people directed their own unresolved pain and hurt toward me.

In the stillness of the night and unguarded waking moments, I still hear the dark echoes of past hurts resonate within me. They chime in self-debasing unison:

"You'll never amount to anything!"

"You're just like your father (mother)!"

"I don't know what's wrong with you!"

"You're an embarrassment to me (us)!"

On and on and on, the dark chorus of voices replay within me, further locking my blistered heart deep into a self-pity prison of despair. In the past, in a false attempt to render these words powerless, I remember sneering or rolling my eyes in contempt. My pretense defensive shield, in retrospect, kept none of the hurtful words from finding their target. I did not realize then that my tender, formative, yet rebellious heart was being impaled by the very powerful sting of each hurtful word.

I now recognize my heart's affliction. It has been a lot longer than twelve years in the woman's account; still, my internal bleeding is horrendous.

Personal Prayer

Now that I've heard this story of hope for the shunned, I, too, choose to peer out of my dark self-pity prison—I sense there is hope for me. I will take my own faith walk and I will reach out and touch you, Jesus with my prayer of faith—for my healing.

Jesus, heal my affliction. For far too long, the enemy of my soul (Satan) has convinced me (through words of others or my own self-debasing actions) that I am not worthy! While the enemy has deceived me and encouraged me to respond to others with a devil-may-care attitude or you-can't-hurt me response, I now realize his goal has been to further entomb me in his dark, demonic embrace.

I further realize that the most deadly cancer is cancer of the heart. A cancer that our enemy attempts to beat into us— one cancerous peg at a time. Demonic pegs that include but are not limited to shame, guilt, anger, fear, bitterness, resentment, self-pity, and unforgiveness. His aim is (and will always be) to paralyze and destroy every child of God and rob us of our true destiny.

I now clearly see the truth of God's Word: "The thief does not come except to steal, and to kill and to destroy. I have come that they may have life, and that they may have it more abundantly" (John 10:10).

Forgive me of my rebellion and especially free me from this self-pity prison of despair. I accept my freedom, based on your truth, dear Jesus—*I am worthy!* I will choose to pray for all the significant and insignificant people in my life who brought words of pain to my heart. I will take a further step of faith and forgive them and pray that they be delivered out of their own prisons.

As I close my simple prayer, I hear a faith whisper in response: "Your faith has made you well. Go in peace and be healed of your affliction."

Thank you, Jesus!

The Pole's Witness

Scripture Passage

Now it happened on a certain day, as He was teaching, that there were Pharisees and teachers of the law sitting by, who had come out of every town of Galilee, Judea, and Jerusalem. And the power of the Lord was present to heal them. Then behold, men brought on a bed a man who was paralyzed, whom they sought to bring in and lay before Him. And when they could not find how they might being him in, because of the crowd, they went up on the housetop and let him down with his bed through the tiling into the midst before Jesus.

When He saw their faith, He said to him, "Man, your sins are forgiven you." And the scribes and the Pharisees began to reason saying, "Who is this who speaks blasphemies" Who can forgive sins but God alone?"

But when Jesus perceived their thoughts, He answered and said to them, "Why are you reasoning in your hearts? Which is easier, to say "Your sins are forgiven you," or to say, 'Rise up and walk'? But that you may know that the Son of Man has power on earth to forgive sins"—He said to the man who was paralyzed, "I say to you arise, take up your bed, and go to your house."

Immediately he rose up before them, took up what he had been lying on, and departed to his own house, glorifying God. And they were all amazed, and they glorified God and were filled with fear, saying, "We have seen strange things today!"

Luke 5:17–26

Blessed Pearl 7 – A Pole Witness

As ordinary, strong, and parallel poles, we serve as key transports for our paralytic owner. We are inserted into four loops on each side of a canvas cot and are united with a common robust rope. Interwoven netting of rope meshed lengthwise completes the support structures we are charged to carry. We and our paralyzed owner share one thing in common. We are both rigidly frozen in form. From the ground, our owner's peripheral vision is extremely limited. He sees approaching people as follows: heads at five feet, waist at two feet, and finally the upright form knees to face at one foot. His limited view changes only slightly when being carried by family or close loyal friends.

On predictable and mundane days, we are held by dedicated hands, transporting our owner to and from a place of alms giving outside the temple. But today the hands that hold us feel different. The supportive hands of friends are infused with faith! A hope-driven faith that is strengthened upon hearing about the healing power of Jesus. Their faith radiates from their heart to their hands to our wooden core. Their faith awakens our true natural tree origin spoken into being by our Creator. Today, we detour from our normal course as a strong shared sense of expectation and faith propels our owner's friends.

The heightened faith conversation of fast-moving friends spills a contagious seed of hope. The seed pierces our owner's cement-like physical prison and lands in his heart. The friends' sandals slow momentarily as we turn down the street to the house where Jesus is teaching. The entrance door is blocked by a multi-tiered crowd pushing and shoving for a spot where even though they can't see Jesus they hope to hear his every word.

Hands shift quickly as one of our carriers redirects his friends beyond the crowd and around to the back of the house. We are set upon the ground as he quickly and excitedly unfolds the plan to his friends. One friend grabs a nearby wooden ladder and sets it parallel to the natural clay steps, which give access to the rooftop from the rear. Next, ropes are secured to our pole ends as we and our owner are raised and set on the rooftop.

A faith-filled friend listens for the direction of Jesus's muffled voice below. He simultaneously counts the outer support beams to arrive at the prime lowering position. With swift crisscross knife slashes, another friend cuts the outer layer of clay, which was poured evenly over sunbaked tiles as a protective rain barrier. The friends pick out the dried layers and throw the puzzle-like pieces tumbling to the back alley. Clay tiles and their supporting reed slats are carefully removed and stacked to the side.

The friends' faith reaches a unified crescendo as the outline of Jesus comes into view. Murmurs of personal discomfort rise from the front row of Jesus's audience as dust particles descend and settle on their heads and clothes. They look up in disdain as they shake the dust from their person, evoking a few nearby sneezes.

Jesus having already sensed the presence of great faith continues teaching, unaffected by the commotion above. Rays of sunlight from the open rooftop brighten the room. In the next moment, we are being lowered alongside our owner between two beams. We hang suspended before the loving and soul-piercing eyes of Jesus. He looks up at the elongated hole in the ceiling and smiles as he acknowledges the friends' faith. Jesus, knowing that a far deeper spiritual paralysis binds our owner's soul, looks intently at him and says, "Man, your sins are forgiven you." The heavy invisible guilt-weight of sin is instantly and miraculous lifted. Tears of gratitude—for unmerited mercy—stream down our owner's face, and our load seems to lighten.

Upon hearing Jesus's sin-absolving words, the faces of scribes and Pharisees contort in unison as each mind processes the common thought, "Who is this who speaks blasphemies? Who can forgive sins but God alone?" Jesus's eyes and attention shift to the row of nearby scribes and Pharisees and verbally exposes their thoughts. He says, "Why are you reasoning in your hearts? Which is easier to say, 'Your sins are forgiven you' or to say, 'Rise up and walk?'" Before their lips could form the obvious answer, Jesus continues, "But that you may know that the Son of Man has power on earth to forgive sins"—he says to the paralyzed man, "I say to you *arise*, take up your bed and go to your house."

As the God-empowered fifth word *arise* is pronounced by Jesus, the second layer of paralysis (physical) is addressed. Our owner's brain receives the miraculous Word as the power of Jesus's Word travels throughout his body, freeing him from his paralysis. He gets up! Ropes drop from the rooftop as friends rejoice above. Every eye in the audience blinks in disbelief, and every lowered jaw reveals an open mouth in awe of this great miracle. Our owner heeds the balance of Jesus's command. He picks us up along with his cot and walks through the crowd which parts like the Red Sea, all the while glorifying God. Once outside, faith-filled friends leap off the roof to join their healed friend as he leads the praise parade home!

Jesus has once again demonstrated his ability to heal anyone and everyone at will totally and completely. It is incontrovertible proof of his deity. The crowd's reaction is mixed: some are truly amazed and rightly glorify God, others more religiously staunch, are curiously noncommittal; not void of wonder and amazement—but utterly void of faith.

Reflection

How many times have friends and loved ones or even strangers brought me before Jesus in prayer? Without my knowledge, they were moved by God's providence to carry me by faith into God's presence.

My God-honoring family and friends saw my spiritual paralysis caused by my own rebellion and sin before I even knew or cared about my own spiritual condition. Although I was convinced that their love for me was genuine, I was equally convinced that since I was more educated and had a broader worldview, I could not be constrained by their simple faith. I was one with the Pharisees—void of faith!

After reading this account, I recognize that I have been so worldly conscious that I have inadvertently blocked my will from having access to God's mercy and grace. I have embraced and defended the popular worldly secularist view with passionate blind allegiance. In ignorance, I have "slapped" the face of God.

I have found profound emptiness, disillusionment, and finally despair at the end of my secularist credo. Although it sounded noble at the beginning and it sustained by own ego and self-worth for a season in life, it has now reached the edges of my own selfish heart and left me paralyzed in the Tower of Me! I cannot manufacture the mercy, compassion, and grace I see in other people's lives and I'm stranded in a desperate and lonely place.

Personal Prayer

Help me to believe, Jesus, that I might seek healing from you for my self-inflicted spiritual paralysis. I now choose to exercise my own free will and nurture the seed of faith that you have divinely deposited in every human heart. Past and current prayers of friends and loved ones, which I now recognize and value, have certainly helped to bring my stubborn, thirsty heart to this place at this time.

Today, I read the following:

> And you He made alive who were dead in trespasses and sins, in which you once walked according to the course of this world, according to the prince of the power of the air (Satan), the spirit who now works in the sons of disobedience, among whom also we all once conducted ourselves in the lusts of our flesh, fulfilling the desire of the flesh and of the mind and were by nature children of wrath, just as the others.
>
> But God, who is rich in mercy, because of His great love with which He loved us, even when we were dead in trespasses, made us alive together with Christ (by grace you have been saved) and raised up together, and made us to sit together in the heavenly places in Christ Jesus that in the ages to come, He might show the exceeding riches of His grace in His kindness toward us in Christ Jesus. For by grace you have been saved through faith and that not of yourselves; it is the gift of God, not of works, lest anyone should boast.

For we are His workmanship, created in Christ Jesus
for good works, which God prepared beforehand that
we should walk in them.

Ephesians 2:1–10

So here I am in need of redemption and healing of my
wayward and sinful heart. I recognize that my internal paralysis was caused by my own sins of rebellion and pride. I ask
you, Jesus, to speak spiritual freedom to my heart, to free
me from my sin paralysis. Forgive me of my sins for they
are many.

By the power of your Word and Holy Spirit, I accept your
free gift of grace and forgiveness in exchange for my sin burden. Thank you for dying on Calvary's cross to free a sin-
laden, paralyzed man like me. Thank you for opening the eyes
of my understanding to see that paralysis of the heart is worse
than paralysis of body. Amen.

Thorn Witness

Scripture Passage

So then Pilate took Jesus and scourged Him. And the soldiers twisted a crown of thorns and put on His head, and they put on Him a purple robe. Then they said, "Hail King of the Jews!" And they struck Him with their hands. Pilate then went out again, and said to them, "Behold, I am bringing Him out to you, that you may know that I find no fault in Him."

Then Jesus came out, wearing the crown of thorns and the purple robe. And Pilate said to them, "Behold the Man!" Therefore, when the Chief Priests and officers saw Him, they cried out, saying, "Crucify Him, crucify Him!" Pilate said to them, "You take Him and crucify Him, for I find no fault in Him." The Jews answered him, "We have a law and according to our law He ought to die, because He made Himself the Son of God."

Therefore, when Pilate heard that saying, he was the more afraid, and went again into the Praetorium, and said to Jesus, "Where are you from?" But Jesus gave him no answer. Then Pilate said to Him, "Are you not speaking to me? Do you not know that I have power to crucify You, and power to release You?" Jesus answered, "You could have no power at all against Me unless it had been given you from above. Therefore the one who delivered Me to you has the greater sin." From then on Pilate sought to release Him, but the Jews cried out saying, "If you let this Man go, you are not Caesar's friend. Whoever makes himself a king speaks against Caesar."

When Pilate therefore heard that saying, he brought Jesus out and sat down in the judgment seat in a place that is called the Pavement. Now it was the Preparation Day of Passover, and about the sixth hour. And he said to the Jews, "Behold your King!" But they cried out, "Away with Him, away with Him! Crucify Him!" Pilate said to them, "Shall I crucify your king?" The chief priests answered, "We have no king but Caesar!" Then he delivered Him to them to be crucified. Then they took Jesus and led Him away.

John 19:1–11

Blessed Pearl 8 – Thorn Witness

Laughing sinisterly, the two Roman soldiers leap across a gully and down to a rock area on their Satan-inspired mission. Their eyes are fixed on a large thorn tree just ahead of them. After six quick steps, their brain, legs, feet, and finally sandals bring them to a stop. One of the soldiers wildly unsheathes his small sword from its leather scabbard, swinging it upward into the Jerusalem air.

With a battle-tested grunt of focused purpose, energy, and anger, he swiftly cuts downward through the air as the edge of his blade severs a large crooked thorn branch. The branch is armed with thorns growing in pairs which are gnarly, curved, cruel, and menacing to guard the tree's olive-like fruit when in season.

Creation memory awakens within the severed branch and travels down to the last thorn and quickens us (the thorns) to witness this account. You see, we profusely multiplied after man first chose to turn his back on the voice of God and his plan for them in the Garden of Eden. I remember God's voice saying to man:

> Cursed is the ground for your sake; in toil you shall eat of it, all the days of your life. Both thorns, and thistles it shall bring forth for you and you shall eat of the herbs of the field.

> Genesis 3:17–19

To avoid pricking themselves, the Roman soldiers carefully use their leather scabbards to bend and twist us into a small circlet. A soldier carries us on the edge of his sword to an interior court. We wonder what purpose we will serve these angry men. We are tilting and sliding downward, on sword edge, landing askew on a man's head. Then with two quick sword whacks, which push and tear us into a forehead and scalp, we're leveled on his head. The mocking laughter of the man's torturers fills the air as a final downward whack, with flat end of the soldier's sword sends us piercing into his head. We are impaled into his head as his blood rushes to surrounds us. We sense a deep knowing love. We are one with Jesus, our Creative Agent.

A purple robe is put on him. The blood of his scourged and flayed body absorbs into the robe material and begins to adhere to his body. I hear my Creator's tormentors yell mockingly, "Hail, King of the Jews!" We, the thorns, are rocked violently back and forth by the pugilistic blows of coarse angry Roman fists, which land painfully on Jesus's face and body.

In the next moments, we are shuffled forward by Jesus's weakened legs and feet. The Roman soldiers prod and shove Jesus. Two distinct and parallel trails of smeared blood on Pilate's floor mark the path behind us. Out in the open air now, crowned on Jesus's head, we come to a standstill. We hear Pilate proclaim to the crowd, "Behold the man." Pilate's calculation that the extreme and vivid scene of a cruelly scourged, thorn-impaled, and blood-drenched Jesus would serve to quell the hatred backfires. Raging hatred still boils in the veins and hearts of the religious mob in the courtyard below. The Satan-inspired Jewish chief priests and their zealous adherents cry out in death determined unison, "Crucify him, crucify him!"

We sit embedded on our Creator's head wondering what enemy has sown the evil seeds of hatred and murder so deeply in men's hearts that they fail to recognize their Creator and Messiah? Like a thick morning fog, the whirling anger and hatred seem to breach the mob's hearts and spill into the surrounding area. They breathe their own hearts' dark air. Perpetual hatred consumes them, inside and out.

In contrast to the evil demonic aura of hate, which engulfs and feeds the mob, we thorns sense the calm and quiet heart of our peaceful Creator holding us up between heaven and earth. The angry and boisterous exchange continues; Pilate adjudicates Jesus as having no fault and the mob salivates determinedly at the prospect of death by cruel crucifixion. Death on the basis that Jesus made himself out to be God. Pilate momentarily feels a twinge of fear as he goes back inside. He then asks three questions of Jesus: "Where are you from?" "Are you not speaking to me?" and "Do you not know that I have power to crucify you and power to release you?" Jesus, looking at Caesar through blood-shot eyes full of love and heavenly authority, responds, "You could have no power at all against me, unless it had been given you from above. Therefore, the one who delivered me to you has the greater sin." Pilate, moved by Jesus's response, seeks ways to release him. The Jews prevail by accusing Pilate of being against Caesar.

Pilate folds upon hearing the anarchist card played. After all, he did report to Caesar. Pilate, having been trumped once, brings Jesus out as he takes his official judgment seat. Pilate then takes a stinging shot at the chief priests as he says, "Behold your King!" The stiff-necked Jewish mob, whose faces are contorted with evil, cry out in vehement hatred, "Away with him, away with him! Crucify Him!" Pilate now smirks gleefully as he says, "Shall I crucify your king?" The chief priests, sensing the opportunity for the final trump, proudly gather their ornate religious robes around their puffed self-righteous chests and say, "We have no king but Caesar!" Pilate, left with no choice, delivers Jesus to be crucified.

Reflection

I now see that the chief priests failed to recognize their own Messiah in spite of the numerous prophecies to the contrary. They selfishly desired a Messiah that would deliver them from Roman rule while keeping themselves in power.

Erroneously, they picked the wrong king and trumped themselves when they said, "We have no king but Caesar!" They had allowed themselves to be deceived to the point where their own religious self-righteousness would only accept a Messiah that would serve them.

If I'm honest with myself, I am at times as stiff-necked in my relationship with you, God, as the chief priests in this account. I may not wear the outer robes of external distinction, but my chameleon-like inner disguises that serve King Me are equally self-serving.

I'm challenged daily to blur and sometimes override the line of Godly conscience you created within me. The world's social secularist gospel says, "It's okay to engage in premarital sex," "It's okay to practice homosexuality," "It's okay to 'choose' to abort my child," "It's okay to (fill in the blank)." In essence, their God-excluding mantra can be summarized as follows: "If it feels good do it. Anyone who disagrees with you is intolerant!" Today as I read Romans 1:18–32, God's truth has been deposited in my heart, and I can no longer serve this humanistic gospel. I am compelled to serve a higher truth—your truth.

I've allowed the world's lies to prick, impale, and hold my mind in a dark vise-like grip. I've allowed myself to be deceived by the satanically inspired messages of doubt, shame, worthlessness, and despair. As part of fallen humanity, I, too, share in driving that awful mocking crown of thorns into Jesus's head, being in complete contempt for all that you love and value.

Personal Prayer

Father, in Jesus's name, forgive me of my sin. May the very thorns multiplied by man's original sin and rebellion in the garden serve to remind me of the holy redemptive act that took place on Calvary's Cross to free me from the curse of sin and eternal death.

Deliver me from this world's satanically inspired deception and restore my Godly conscience.

I now realize that on the day when the crown of thorns separated heaven and earth on Jesus's head, provision was made for me to escape my thorns of shame and guilt so that I myself could one day wear the crown of life and glory, you purchased for me at Calvary. As the Bible records in James 1:12, "Blessed is the man who endures temptation; for when he has been approved, he will receive the *Crown Of Life* which the Lord has promised to those who love Him."

I thank you, Father, in Jesus's name for delivering me from my sin and rebellion. Create in me a new heart and renew a right spirit within me. Amen!

A Crossbeam Witness

Scripture Passage

There were also two others, criminals, led with Him to be put to death. And when they had come to the place called Calvary, they crucified Him, and the criminals, one on the right hand and the other on the left. Then Jesus said, "Father, forgive them, for they do not know what they do."

And they divided His garments and cast lots. And the people stood looking on, but even the rulers with them sneered, saying, "He saved others; let him save Himself if He is the Christ, the chosen of God." The soldiers also mocked Him, coming and offering Him sour wine and saying, "If you are the King of the Jews, save yourself." And an inscription also was written over Him in letters of Greek, Latin, and Hebrew: This is Jesus King of the Jews.

Then one of the criminals who were hanged blasphemed Him saying, "If You are the Christ, save Yourself and us." But the other, answering rebuked him, saying, "Do you not even fear God, seeing you are under the same condemnation? And we indeed justly, for we receive the due reward of our deeds; but this Man has done nothing wrong." Then he said to Jesus, "Lord, remember me when You come into your kingdom." And Jesus said to him, "Assuredly, I say to you, today you will be with Me in Paradise."

Now it was about the sixth hour, and there was darkness over all the earth until the ninth hour. Then the sun was darkened, and the veil of the temple was torn in two. And when Jesus had cried out with a loud voice, He said, "Father into Your hands I commit My Spirit." Having said this, He breathed His last. So when the centurion saw what had happened, he glorified God, saying, "Certainly this was a righteous Man!" And the whole crowd who came together to that sight, seeing what had been done, beat their breasts and returned. But all His acquaintances, and the women who followed Him from Galilee, stood at a distance, watching these things.

Luke 23:32–49

Blessed Pearl 9 – The Crossbeam Witness

Once a proud majestic tree, I now yield to the cutter's axe as I crash with a heavy thud on the forest floor. The impact sends a rippling tremor under my cutter's feet, rattling his body from feet to chattering teeth. I sense other cutters advance as they join in a mass debranching of my once proud torso. They quickly rough cut and axe-shape me into rough timber for sale on the open market. As a piece of timber cut by an apprentice, I find myself in the low grade pile, not fit for building.

For an extended time, I'm ignored and left to dry in the dusty pile. Today, a cruel supplier of crucifixion crosses buys me to maintain his every dwindling inventory. Rome's appetite for crucifixion examples these days cannot be satisfied. No one is allowed to challenge or undermine Rome's authority!

As a shorter piece of timber, I'm chosen as the cross beam: notched at half-point and eventually joined to a taller timber notched at top side to form a robust cross at the crucifixion site. I overhear the impatient coarse and demanding voice of a Roman soldier bark, "We need three more crosses now!" Along with two other cross beams and corresponding tall timbers, we're loaded and carted to our destination.

As the first cross beam unloaded I'm dragged along a stoned pathway. A Roman soldier's eyes sift through the crowd as he reaches out and grabs a strong Cyrenian man named Simon and places me on his shoulders. From atop his shoulders, I see a bloodied, thorn-crowned, and extremely tortured man leaving a trail of blood immediately ahead of us (Luke 23:26). Every time the man ahead of me stumbles and falls, a Roman whip cracks upon his body as they jerk him upright and push him forward to Calvary. Upon arrival at Calvary, two Roman soldiers grab my crossbeam, releasing me from Simon's shoulders. Another soldier jerks, stumbling Simon, spits at him, and shoves him aside with disdain, as he mumbles, "Stupid foreigners!"

I'm dropped heavily on the ground, sending a thundering and teetering echo into Calvary's death-stenched air. I'm joined, notch to notch, to a taller timber to form a cruel cross, the preferred evil form of Roman torture and punishment. The bloodied, tortured body of the leading man is slammed and dragged across my beam forcing wooden splinters deep into his body. Instantly, I sense vibrations of intense love and knowledge as deep creative memory surges through me. This is no ordinary man, this is my Creative Agent, Jesus Christ! Something is going terribly wrong!

Seasoned evil hands of angry and torturous men roughly grab and yank Jesus's hands and feet and splay them onto my wooden surface, sending forced blood spatters into my wooden pores. Cruelly, they pound rusty nails through Jesus's hands and feet, forcing his skin and pieces of tendons at rusty nail tip, into the core of my wood. I am now one with my Creator. I'm jerked upright by Roman soldiers and dropped with a pounding force into a death hole. I hear the mocking laughter of Roman soldiers and chief priests in the crowd as the flesh and bones of Jesus's hands and feet are torn against me. I totter from side to side as rocks are crammed around death's hole to secure the bloody cross.

I feel Jesus press against me in excruciating pain as he says, "Father, forgive them, for they do not know what they do." His words are meant not only for the Roman soldiers used as implements of torture, but for the entirety of mankind. His words seem to fall on deaf ears as Roman soldiers cast lots at the base of the cross for his garments. The Jewish chief priests and rulers, still standing entombed in their stiff-necked self-righteousness, sneeringly say, "He saved others, let him save himself if he is the Christ, the chosen of God." Roman soldiers join the chorus as they mockingly chime in, saying, "If you are the King of the Jews, save yourself." I feel another nail drive into the upright beam, securing a sign that reads: *This is Jesus, King of the Jews.*

Another blasphemous voice cuts through the dank Calvary atmosphere, spouting, "If you are the Christ, save yourself and us." The heavy air is momentarily parted as the repentant faith-driven voice of the second criminal says, "Do you not even fear God, seeing you are under the same condemnation? And we indeed justly, for we receive the due reward of our deeds, but this Man has done nothing wrong." Then he said to Jesus, "Lord, remember me when you come into your kingdom." Jesus acknowledges the criminal's repentant heart and responds with the promise, "Assuredly, I say to you, today you will be with me in paradise."

As I support my Creator and Savior of the world, I hear mercy, forgiveness, and grace in his voice. I somehow know that this repentant criminal is but one, of many more to come, who will be absolved of sin, set spiritually free, and be given eternal life.

Suddenly, mankind's darkest day, which would yet become his brightest, is enshrouded in total darkness throughout all the earth. Meanwhile, the veil of the temple in Jerusalem is being torn top to bottom. A veil that represents limited access to God, via the High Priest, is torn asunder and unlimited access to God is established through the torn sacrificial body of Jesus Christ, Mediator and Redeemer of all mankind.

I feel Jesus's final press into me as he says, "Father, into your hands I commit my spirit." He then lets go of his last breath. A Roman centurion (commander of a hundred soldiers) hears the initial echo of Christ's first words resound in his now awestruck and pliable heart. "Father, forgive them, for they do not know what they do." The centurion unashamedly cries out, "Certainly this was a righteous man!" (Mark 15:34 says, "This was the Son of God.")

As the crossbeam holding God's perfect sacrifice for the sins of all mankind, I stretch out infinitely to all mankind to beckon them to accept the free gift of eternal salvation. As I am given a blessed review of my family tree history, I recall three distinct moments where we were called upon to uphold Jesus. As a feed trough, we cradled him at birth. As a wind-and sea-tossed boat, we cradled his tired body. Finally, in the form of a rugged cross, I now cradle the Perfect Sacrifice of God.

It is here in the fullness of God's time where Christ paid the price for man's sin and provided the free gift of eternal life. A free gift provided by the Father, through his Son, to bring fallen mankind by faith back into a perfect loving relationship with him. Death will not prevail but will soon be eternally defeated as Christ rises from the dead: the Perfect Sacrifice (see next and final chapter).

Reflection

As I honestly review my life, I realize that I have vacillated between times of simple faith and complex secular nonbelief. Until now, I have been truly ignorant of the price Jesus Christ paid on the cross for the penalty of my sin. I now see that God's holy justice demands righteous judgment and I am doomed to eternal separation from God. I may not have sneered and mocked you openly like the soldiers and self-righteous religious leaders. But the deafening silence of failing to acknowledge your loving hand on my life, even in my rebellion, surely rivals the mockers at the foot of the cross. The truth of Romans 5:8 has brought hope to my sinful heart, where the Bible states, "But God demonstrates His own love towards us; in that while we were still sinners Christ died for us."

I have exhausted myself trying to be good. Religious performance has left me exhausted, full of guilt and doubt, and as empty as the Grand Canyon. Your love isn't based on my ability to be good and somehow balance my bad. I realize now that like the repentant thief, I must come by faith alone, bringing *nothing* but my sinful heart darkened and encrusted with guilt and shame. I repent of my sin and ask for your forgiveness. Your Word does perfectly state, "For by grace you have been saved through faith, and that not of yourself; it is a gift of God, not works, lest anyone should boast" (Ephesians 2:8–9).

I have come to realize that your Word reveals perfect truth and has broken my religious performance yoke, which in the past has only served to increase my guilt and contribute to my spiritual despair. A spiritual despair that can be likened to a dark sinister vortex of guilt and shame keeping me in a prison of spiritual poverty. In this dark hopeless prison of isolation and despair, the enemy convinced me that God's love was not for me.

Personal Prayer

Today, dear God, I choose to accept the free gift of grace and forgiveness you have provided for me. I exchange my sinfulness for your righteousness, and I thank you for the restoration you bring to my life and the secure promise of eternal life. I thank you, Father, for Jesus Christ's sacrifice on the cross for my freedom. I realize now that it was your love for lost mankind that held Jesus on the cross and not the rusty Roman nails.

More importantly, it was *for me*. Today, I have heard the echo of Christ's Word resonate in my own heart, "Father, forgive them, for they do not know what they do." It wasn't only for the self-righteous religious leaders and the Roman soldiers that you spoke those words. You were mercifully looking through time and space for all sinners and *you saw me in bondage to sin* and you made forgiveness available for me.

I now choose to exercise my free will as I ask you to forgive me of my sins. Deliver me from my pride and stubbornness, which has kept me from experiencing your tender mercies and grace. I accept your sacrifice as full payment for all my sin, and I invite Jesus Christ into my heart. Thank you for creating a new heart in me and filling me with your Holy Spirit. Amen!

A Stone Witness

Now behold, there was a man named Joseph, a council member, a good and just man. He had not consented to their decision and deed. He was from Arimathea, a city of the Jews, who himself was also waiting for the kingdom of God. This man went to Pilate and asked for the body of Jesus. Then he took it down, wrapped it in linen, and laid it in a tomb that was hewn out of the rock, where no one had ever laid before.

Matthew 28:1–10

Now after the Sabbath, as the first day of the week began to dawn, Mary Magdalene and the other Mary came to see the tomb. And behold, there was a great earthquake; for an Angel of the Lord descended from heaven, and came and rolled back the stone from the door, and sat on it.

His countenance was like lightning and his clothing as white as snow. And the guards shook for fear of him, and became like dead men. But the angel answered and said to the women, "Do not be afraid, for I know that you seek Jesus who was crucified. He is not here; for He is risen, as He said. Come; seen the place where the Lord lay. And go quickly and tell His disciples that He is risen from the dead, and indeed

He is going before you into Galilee; there you will see Him. Behold, I have told you."

So they went out quickly from the tomb with fear and great joy, and ran to bring His disciples word. And as they went to tell His disciples, behold, Jesus met them, saying, "Rejoice!" So they came and held Him by the feet and worshiped Him. Then Jesus said to them, "Do not be afraid. Go and tell My brethren to go to Galilee, and there they will see Me.

Luke 23:50–53

Blessed Pearl 10 – Tombstone Witness

As a new tomb perfectly cut to cradle the shape of a human body, I belong to Joseph of Arimathea, a rich and prominent Jewish man. Like most tombs of my time, I reside in a former stone quarry. I'm unique in that I have a circular rolling stone at my entrance. Only the rich can afford the added labor and cost of a round-shaped cut stone.

Earlier today, I felt a powerful earthquake—epicenter Calvary—followed by an ominous darkness. All of God's creation was enshrouded in total blackness for a space of three hours. Our God put mankind and creation on high alert! But, I ponder, for what reason?

Suddenly, at my entrance, I hear the shuffling Judean sandals of Joseph my owner. As he approaches me, a tear travels down his face and drops on my stone surface. It's wet, quiet echo resounds through my hollow chamber. I'm momentarily warmed by the tear as I sense the enormous grief and love that my master feels for him who is carried in his arms. He leans over me as he gently and lovingly lowers the linen-wrapped body into my stone cavity.

I hear the slow crushing grind of small pebbles as the rolling stone closes and total darkness envelops my interior cave like space. Darkness and the grave temporarily rule for two days and nights. When the second night succumbs to the third day, God's divine resurrection power suddenly explodes through time, space, and my small tomb!

God's miraculous life-giving power instantly emanates from Christ, enabling him to take up his own life. Christ is risen!

"My God, my Creator," I cry out! I realize that I have been tending the body of Jesus Christ.

I hear the dark, sinister, and demonic evil shrieking echoes of death, hell, and the grave as they flee in final defeat, unable to hold the Son of God! In a God-affirming majestic and miraculous nanosecond, I'm left with nothing but crumpled linen (still wrapped) and the circular stone still closing my entrance. Christ has defeated Satan, death, and the grave.

The divine stark contrast of Jesus's ability to raise the dead (Lazarus account) and raising himself through his Father's shared will and power overwhelms me. Lazarus had been raised from the dead *after the stone had been rolled away* and upon Jesus's command, "Lazarus, come forth!" Lazarus exited the grave still bound hand and foot in his grave clothes and with his face wrapped in cloth. Jesus then said, "Loose him and let him go." You see, Jesus never attended a funeral without bringing the dead back to life.

Meanwhile, outside the tomb, I hear the faint delicate sound of women's sandals. Suddenly, another great earthquake hits—epicenter me—sending tremulous ripples throughout my space. Heavenly light again floods my hollow space. God's heavenly messenger, the angel of the Lord descends, rolls back my entrance stone door and sits on it! From my vantage point, I see the angel of the Lord radiating like lightning with clothes as white as snow.

The guards, which the chief priests had placed at the door, are recovering their balance from the earthquake, only to experience the divine shaking of the angel's presence. They fall to the ground in a chorus of thuds, unconscious with fear. Outside, I see two women standing amid the group of unconscious guards whose haphazard bodies now blanket the grass still soaked with early morning dew.

The angel of the Lord says to the woman, "Do not be afraid for I know that you seek Jesus who was crucified. He is not here for he is risen as he said. Come, see the place where the Lord lay. And go quickly and tell his disciples that he is risen from the dead, and indeed, he is going before you into Galilee, there you will see him. Behold, I have told you."

The two women, faces still radiant from the angel's holy aura, respond to his invite to look inside my empty tomb. The powerful words of the Lord's angel echoes again in their hearts, "He is not here, he is risen!" Their hearts confirm the holy echo of God's Word as they quickly exit with great awe and joy. They step over the unconscious guards as they break into a sandal-flapping run to tell Jesus's disciples what they have seen and heard. The sound of their footsteps subsides in the distance, and I hear the risen Jesus say to them: "Rejoice!"

Jesus's Word resonates into my stone cavity where I now hold the precious memory of the Risen Christ. With a surge of God's creation energy, I cry out, "Hosanna, Christ is risen!" I immediately recall my stone history past when Jesus said, "I tell you that if these (the multitude) should keep silent the stones would immediately cry out" (Luke 19:40).

Reflection

My past moral failures have multiplied and burdened my heart with an unbearable sin load.

Fear, shame, and guilt gave birth to unbelief, which served as my dark captor.

The enemy of my soul succeeded in driving me into a twice hollow and dark cave of mental depression.

I unconsciously allow myself to stay encased in my own false, protective, and deceptive tomb. I allow my own negativity and that of other sinister people close to me to wound, warp, and wrap my heart in death's suffocating darkness.

I permit the world's psychobabble practice—"blame everyone but yourself"—to make me the *perfect victim.* The dark and deadly result is that I have become the imperfect yet perfectly entombed victim—with no way out! I am in need of resurrection!

Personal Prayer

Jesus, through this story, you have opened my spiritual eyes to see the dark, invisible, deceptive, deadly, and stench-ridden clothes, which I falsely believed would protect me.

This self-inflicted entombment enabled by the deceptive lies of Satan has only served to snuff out the real me and has left me a walking dead person.

I accept the blame and responsibility for so quickly accepting the world's solution by believing myself to be a helpless victim. Jesus, I realize that you paid the perfect sacrificial price for the redemption of all victims for all time. I ask you now to forgive me of my sin and destroy the chains that bind me and resurrect me!

I come believing the promise in your Word: "Come to Me, all who are weary and heavy-laden, and I will give you rest. Take My yoke upon you, and learn from Me, for I am gentle and humble in heart; and you shall find rest for your souls. For My yoke is easy, and My load is light" (John 11:27–30).

By faith, I exchange my unholy suffocating grave clothes for the righteousness of Christ, which you promised me. I hear your gentle, loving and freeing holy whisper resonate in my heart, "Loose him (her) and let him (her) go!" Thank you, Jesus, for resurrecting me! Amen!

Postscript

At book publish time (Dec. 2013), I am three years cancer free. All of my CT scans and blood panels show that I am cancer free—thank you, God! I also know that if my outcome would have been different, I would still say, "Thank you, God!"

My first chemotherapy session (October 2010) had left me looking like a Nazi Jewish death camp internee. Physically, my external body looked hollow, frail, wispy, almost lacking life. Internally, my physical organs, blood stream, and unseen parts were being throttled by the chemo solution sent traveling through my body to kill the cancer cells.

So this ending in some way goes back to the beginning. If I could have seen but one of the benefits for myself and others who went through this process with me, I would have gladly chosen to go through the trial, if it simply yielded the letter of faith below.

As I poured over the many encouraging e-mails after the first chemo session, one particularly stands out—it is from my son and it reads (unedited) as follows:

> Date: Tue, November 9, 2010 9:25 am
> From: Dean Chavez
> To: Felipe Chavez
> Subj: I love you
>
> I love you pops!! I am sorry you have to go thru this…
> but as we know God has a plan for everything. Our

little pea brains can't comprehend the big picture that God sees, so that is when our faith kicks in and we put our lives in 'God-Auto Pilot.'

You have always been the rock for me, the family, extended family and lots of friends. I think as much as you find yourself asking God what it is he wants to come of all this... I think the same thing is going on with everyone within and around the circle of Felipe. As you have mentioned in the past we all need our own direction and faith... counting on someone else's faith, gets you nowhere, no matter how strong their connection is to God.

I see it no different than when an army follows their leader into battle just to end up having that leader become ill or possibly die by the sword. What does the army do then? Do they drop their swords and run because all their faith was caught up in their leader? Or do they rely on their own inner strength, grab their sword and finish the job.

I know this may sound weird to some... but I am at peace with all this... Don't get me wrong... it saddens me that you have to go thru this but I find strength and hope in knowing you are completely grounded in God's grace. I can't imagine going thru this if a family member does not know God... that would be horrifying.

I probably don't tell you Thank you and I Love you quite enough...but I really, really do love you and appreciate everything you do for me and for my family. You have always been my Dad, best friend, buddy, brother, rock… the list goes on and on…

Keep your eye on the prize… God is looking over you and loves you more than anyone on this earth ever can. Take care, get well.

Was my cancer battle worth it? Yes, for it yielded much spiritual fruit. I am truly a blessed man!